THE FORCE *of* FAITH

KENNETH COPELAND

JESUS IS LORD

KENNETH COPELAND
PUBLICATIONS

Unless otherwise noted, all scripture is from the *King James Version* of the Bible.

The Force of Faith

ISBN-10 0-938458-14-0   30-0004
ISBN-13 978-0-938458-14-2

23 22 21 20 19 18   28 27 26 25 24 23

© 1983 Eagle Mountain International Church Inc. aka
Kenneth Copeland Publications

Kenneth Copeland Publications
Fort Worth, TX 76192-0001

For more information about Kenneth Copeland Ministries, visit
kcm.org or call 1-800-600-7395 (U.S. only) or +1-817-852-6000.

1

The Forces of the Re-Created Human Spirit

This I say then, Walk in the Spirit, and ye shall
not fulfil the lust of the flesh. For the flesh lusteth
against the Spirit, and the Spirit against the flesh:
and these are contrary the one to the other: so
that ye cannnot do the things that ye would.... If
we live in the Spirit, let us also walk in the Spirit"
(Galatians 5:16-17, 25).

Romans 8:6 tells us that to be carnally minded is
death. The carnal mind is the mind not regulated by the
Word of God. You will either be obedient to the lusts of
the flesh or to the Word of God.

The word *flesh* used in this scripture simply means
the "body, the five physical senses." If you fulfill the lusts
of the flesh, it will kill you. This statement is blunt but
true. If you are going to mind the things of the flesh,
or walk after its dictates, then death will be the result.
(When I say flesh, many think I am talking about sex, but
sex is only a small part of the five-physical-sense realm.)

"For the flesh lusteth against the Spirit, and the Spirit against the flesh: and these are contrary the one to the other: so that ye cannot do the things that ye would." In the Greek text there are no capital letters. The word *spirit* has been capitalized here at the privilege of the English translators. You need to know this scripture is not speaking primarily of the Holy Spirit but of your spirit. The Holy Spirit has not been sent to lust against your flesh. He lusts against no one, not even the devil. He is not warring against the devil. Jesus did that and left Satan defeated. That war is over! The Holy Spirit has been sent to help you. He is your teacher, comforter, advocate, standby, intercessor, helper. His role is not to dominate, but to assist you.

The reborn human spirit was re-created to rule over the human system. "And the very God of peace sanctify you wholly; and I pray God your whole spirit and soul and body be preserved blameless unto the coming of our Lord Jesus Christ" (1 Thessalonians 5:23). Paul prayed that God would sanctify you completely—spirit, soul and body. It does not say, "body, soul and spirit." The Bible never speaks of the reborn man in this order. But if you listen carefully, you will hear people quote this verse, "body, soul and spirit." Test yourself and find out where you are in your own thinking. If you have them in the wrong order, change and renew your mind now to spirit, soul and body.

To be a powerful Christian, your spirit, trained in the Word, must be in command of your mind and body. The chain of command is spirit (heart), soul (mind, will and emotions), and body (flesh). The words *spirit* and *heart* can be used interchangeably as can the words *soul* and *mind, body* and *flesh.* Your mind should obey what your heart tells it to do, and your heart should be trained by the Holy Spirit in line with the Word of God. The human system works perfectly in this order.

The Apostle Paul, by the Holy Spirit, is saying that the flesh lusts or drives against the spirit (the human spirit, the reborn spirit of a man) and the spirit against the flesh. The spirit demands that the flesh obey and the flesh is reluctant to give up its control. Before a man is born again, his flesh (body) completely dominates his life and will continue to do so unless his mind is renewed by God's Word. "For the word of God is quick, and powerful, and sharper than any twoedged sword, piercing even to the dividing asunder of soul and spirit, and of the joints and marrow..." (Hebrews 4:12). Only the Word can put the spirit, soul and body of a man into proper order.

Paul said, "With my spirit I serve God." (See Romans 7:22.) He is speaking of the spirit on the inside of him who was doing his best to please God. His flesh was trying to continue living unrestrained and unregulated as it had the freedom to do for years.

When a man's mind is not renewed to the New Testament, his spirit is trying to follow the leadership of the Holy Spirit and his body and mind are attempting to live as they always have, following after the world's order of things. He is being pulled in two directions at once. When the man is born again, his spirit becomes a new creature in Christ Jesus, but his mind and body are unchanged. Now his spirit is right with God but *his mind and body must be trained.*

Galatians 5:18-21 says, "But if ye be led of the Spirit, ye are not under the law. Now the works of the flesh are manifest, which are these; Adultery, fornication, uncleanness, lasciviousness, idolatry, witchcraft, hatred, variance, emulations, wrath, strife, seditions, heresies, envyings, murders, drunkenness, revellings, and such like...." Why does the flesh have a desire to do such things? Is it bound to stay that way forever? The devil would like for us to believe so. Then we would be continually combating our flesh and leave him alone.

Your flesh is not evil. It has no nature of its own. It is controlled by some other force—either good or evil. It cannot even live without your spirit. When the spirit leaves the body, the body instantly falls over, lifeless. It is nothing but a bag of meat and bones. It has no life of its own but draws its life from the spirit within it.

"For every one that useth milk is unskilful in the word of righteousness: for he is a babe. But strong meat belongeth to them that are of full age, even those who by reason of use have their senses exercised to discern both good and evil" (Hebrews 5:13-14). This scripture proves even though an area of temptation may not be removed, the flesh can be trained so it will respond to God and the things of God, rather than leaping off into sin at every opportunity.

For example, I am not having any trouble with the devil tempting me to steal, commit adultery or to get drunk. My body no longer craves to do these things. The temptations Satan sends my way now are much more deceptive and sometimes one of them gets by me and I miss it. But thank God, we have an Advocate at the right hand of the Father! When I do miss it I say, "Father, I missed it. I confess that as a sin. I receive my forgiveness in the Name of Jesus." Then I determine that I will not make the same mistake twice. Satan will never get me with that again. I take authority over that problem area in the Name of Jesus with the Word of God.

You must train your flesh to discern between good and evil. You are not bound to an ugly, sinful body nor do you have two natures inside you. God did not create you a spiritual schizophrenic. Your body is not you. Your spirit is you. You *are* a spirit, you have a soul, and you live in a body. Do you have a human? No, you *are* a human. That body is not you—it's where *you* live. If *you* will stand up on the inside, feed your spirit with the Word of God, and renew your mind, your body will just tag along and do what it's told. In fact, it will straighten itself up and begin to function properly.

"And they that are Christ's have crucified the flesh with the affections and lusts" (Galatians 5:24). "This I say then, Walk in the Spirit, and ye shall not fulfil the lust of the flesh" (Galatians 5:16). When the Christian enters the area of walking in the spirit, where he can crucify his flesh and put it under the dominion of his spirit, he begins to know what peace is all about—*to be spiritually minded is life and peace.*

Romans 12:1-2 says, "...brethren...present your bodies a living sacrifice...unto God.... And be not conformed to this world: but be ye transformed by the renewing of your mind." Your mind is a marvelous instrument created by God to retain the things you put into it. It is merely a computer—the most highly organized and finest ever created. But, it was not made to be man's governing system. The mind gives forth information that has been put into it, as does any other computer. When placed in ascendancy over the human system, many times it cannot continue to function, but will break under pressure. It will snap when it has had an overload of responsibility. The mind simply was not created to be lord over the spirit.

The mind can fail in this position but the reborn spirit will not fail. It can take the position of lordship over the human system and operate and maintain the mind and the body. The spirit of a man is designed to accomplish this job successfully.

When you get your system in proper sequence, with your mind renewed to the Word of God so it thinks in line with the New Testament, it takes the pressure off your mind. It can then perform as the carefully pro-grammed computer it really is. You call on it, it gets the scripture, shifts into gear and tells the body, "The Word says we are healed! You get yourself straightened up. You're not to operate in sickness." The body does what it is told and receives healing.

It takes some effort and time to get your mind this well-programmed with the Word. In the Scripture, this process is called *renewing the mind*. Once your mind is renewed to think and respond in line with God's Word, it refuses to accept anything contrary to that Word.

There are four major forces in the reborn human
spirit. They are the force of faith, the force of righteousness, the force of wisdom and the force of love. Galatians
5:22-23 outlines the *fruit* of the spirit: "But the fruit of
the Spirit is love, joy, peace, longsuffering, gentleness,
goodness, faith, meekness, temperance: against such there
is no law." The fruit of the spirit comes under one or
more of these four major forces.

The force of faith is born into your spirit. Under-
girding it is the force of patience. You could almost
say that it is the fifth major force. Actually the force of
patience is a very important, integral part of the force of
faith. In the New Testament, faith and patience are almost
always mentioned together. They are "power twins."

The Force of Faith

Faith is not the product of reason. Do you remember
in Matthew 16:6 Jesus told His men to beware of the
leaven of the Pharisees? They could not understand what
He meant and He asked, "Why do you reason among
yourselves?" They missed what He was saying by trying
to figure it out mentally. They were reasoning.

Men say, "We are reasonable men. We are logical
men, and what you are saying doesn't make sense. It's

not logical." Believers are not to be led by logic. We are not even to be led by "good sense." I have had my sense changed around to where it is good, but what the world calls good sense is not good at all. It is *bad* sense corrupted by Satan, the god of this world. If you want to find out what God thinks, take what the world thinks and reverse it. The world says "seeing is believing." God says "believing is seeing."

Logic is the product of reasoning through the avenues of hearing, tasting, seeing, feeling and smelling. Reasoning is based on the failure in the earth through Satan. Faith is the product of God's Word revealed by His Spirit and is based on the success of the Father in heaven.

The ministry of Jesus was never governed by logic or reason. Jairus fell at the feet of Jesus and said, "My little daughter lieth at the point of death...come and lay thy hands on her...and she shall live" (Mark 5:23). Reason would have said, "I'm sorry. I wish that there was some-thing I could do." Reason operates under the handicap of having no answer to critical needs. The request of this man was *un*reasonable, but Jesus answered him not a word and started toward his house.

On the way to Jairus' house He met another unrea-sonable personality—the little woman with the issue of blood. She had been to many physicians, but continued to grow worse. The doctors had reasoned that she was sick, but their logic had no cure to stop the flow of blood. Understand that I am not criticizing doctors. The doctor is a man's best friend if the man doesn't know how to use his faith. Without doctors most Christians would have died! They have not known how to use their faith. Doctors are fighting the same destroyer we are. They are operating in the realm of the physical, we are operating in the realm of the spirit. They treat disease, we go to the root of the problem and deal with the enemy who causes disease.

This little woman said, "If I may touch but his clothes, I shall be whole" (Mark 5:28). There is no logic in that, is there? It just doesn't make good sense. Reason would have answered, "Hey lady, what's the matter with you? There is a little girl dying down here. I have to go see her. Let go of My clothes." If Jesus had been ruled by *common sense* as most of the Church has been in the past, He would have said, "Folks, let's back off here a minute. We haven't had the morning devotion. We haven't sung number 246 or 391. Nobody has taken up the offering yet. Turn loose of My clothes, lady, for goodness' sake! We can't fool with you now. After all, you have already been to the doctor and he said there was no hope. What can *I* do for you? Go on." Common sense will keep you bound when it is time to act in faith on God's Word!

Look at Jesus. He was not led by logic. He was not led by the mind. He stopped and asked, "Who touched me?" (Mark 5:31). Power had gone out of Him to heal and dry up the issue of blood—not reasoning power, but spiritual power. He said, "Daughter, your faith has made you whole." Her faith caused the power of God to flow into her body and make her whole. That healing was not the product of reason but the product of faith.

Common-sense religion will tell you not to get your hopes up. God heals some people, but it might not be His will to heal you. That sounds *reasonable,* but it never gets results. You will always be the one whom it is not His will to heal. This approach to healing will not work because it is contrary to what the Word of God says. We are talking about being led by the Spirit, not by the common-sense world, not by the logical world. The Holy Spirit will turn you in the opposite direction from the way the world is going but, thank God, He *will* lead you in the direction God is going. All you have to do is be like old Jairus. He didn't care what anyone thought. In fact, in Mark 5 when the man came and told him, "Your little daughter is dead," he didn't say a word. He had already said what he had to say: "Lay your hands on my daughter, and she will live." Jesus turned and said to him, "Just believe." Jairus refused to be moved by what he heard—his *sense* of hearing. There was someone giving him the news that his daughter was dead, but in his heart there was a presence of a power stronger than the bad report. Something in his heart was saying, *I don't care what they say. This is so. I know it is so. I just know what I know! I refuse to give up.* That *something* in his heart was *faith.*

What was controlling the ministry of Jesus? The force of *faith.* And it was not entirely the force of His own faith. His own faith responded to the faith of the people. (It still does.) In Nazareth He could do no mighty works because of unbelief. The people refused to believe. But on the other hand, the little woman's faith stopped Him in His tracks. Jairus' faith moved Him, and Jesus used His faith to raise Jairus' little girl. What was the result of Jairus' faith? He received his daughter back again from the dead. Unreasonable! Illogical! But that is victory of the highest order.

When you need more than just common-sense results, faith is the only way you will get them.

The Bible does not say, "Come, let us reason together, men." It does say, "Come now, and let us reason together, saith the Lord" (Isaiah 1:18). Reasoning with God is different than reasoning with men. God says, "Trust in the Lord with all thine heart; and lean not unto thine own understanding" (Proverbs 3:5). When men reason together it is based on fear. Reasoning outside of the Word is always based on fear. Reasoning from men's minds, men's emotions and men's feelings is determined by fear because the world we live in is operating on the force of fear. The Lord spoke to me while I was preparing this message and said, *The definition of reasoning outside the Word is "worry."* When you begin to reason outside God's Word, you automatically begin to worry. "What if that happens? What are we going to do if the Holy Ghost does break out in our denomination and people start talking in tongues right in the middle of church? What am I going to do?" The big *I*. That is selfishness. The root of selfishness is fear.

Faith is not the product of reason but of the reborn human spirit. It is not the product of the mind but of the heart. Faith is a power force. It is a tangible force, a conductive force. It will move things. Faith will change things. Faith will change the human body. It will change the human mind. It will change the human heart. Faith will change circumstances.

Let's look at fear—the negative side of the coin. Fear is not a mental force. It is a spiritual force, and I'll tell you where it came from.

God created a man called Adam, and gave this man faith. Adam was called the son of God because he was born of God. God created his physical body from the dust of the earth, but that body had no life in it. It was just meat and bones. Then God breathed into Adam the breath or spirit of life. God's spirit was breathed into Adam. This man's life came from inside God. He was a magnificent, powerful creature. With his faith he had dominion over the forces of nature. He had dominion over everything that walked, crawled, swam and moved.

This same man committed high treason, bowing his knee to a spiritual outlaw. By doing so, he gave the vast authority to rule the earth that God had given him into the hands of Satan, and when he did, spiritual death moved into his spirit. The life of God departed and the life of his new god overcame him. Everything about him was perverted. *The faith force born into Adam when God breathed His life into him was perverted and turned into the force we know and recognize as fear.* Fear ruled Adam from that moment, and the first words from his mouth were, "I was afraid."

Fear is a tangible force. Will it change the human body? Jesus said that men's hearts would fail them because of fear of what is coming on the earth. It will change the color of a man's hair and the color of a man's skin. Fear will change his physical body. It will make him sick. Fear will make him conform to the world. It will control his mind. Fear will kill his body.

Fear activates Satan the way faith activates God. Why does the world not accept the logic that if fear, a spiritual force, will make a man sick, then faith, the opposite spiritual force, will make him well? If the force of fear can imprison a man, then the force of faith can make him free. Why do men have confidence in fear and not in faith? They are reasoning *outside* the Word of God and *inside* the world's order. On the other hand, we are reasoning in the world of the spirit by the Word of God.

You Have Faith

"For by grace are ye saved through faith; and that not of yourselves: it is the gift of God" (Ephesians 2:8). Everything in this verse is the gift of God. The grace is the gift of God, the salvation is the gift of God, and the faith to receive salvation is the gift of God. The faith that was imparted to you is God's own faith. It is not of yourself. It is not a human or psychological faith.

"For I say, through the grace given unto me, to every man that is among you, not to think of himself more highly than he ought to think; but to think soberly, according as God hath dealt to every man the measure of faith" (Romans 12:3). Men have quoted this verse and said every man on earth has faith, but this scripture places a qualification on this measure of faith. "For I say, through the grace given unto me (To whom is he speaking?), to every man that is among you." He was not talking to everyone in Rome. His letter was written to Christians.

Second Thessalonians 3:2 simply says, "...for all men have not faith." Not every man in the world has the God kind of faith, but every *born-again* man has this world-overcoming faith. Psychological, human faith or confidence is gained through the mind and experience. It is a confidence in material things that would believe, for example, that, "I will sit on this chair and it will not collapse." This is not the faith we are discussing.

God's faith that the Bible is talking about is imparted to you by Him and resides within your spirit. It is in there to be developed and used in your daily life. Galatians 3:11 says that we are to live by it: "The just shall live by faith" (Romans 1:17). God has given you this powerful faith to sustain you in this life. It is so powerful, even a measure as big as a mustard seed can pluck up a mountain and throw it into the sea. (See Mark 11:22-24.)

Every man who has received the new birth—who has been born again and made Jesus the Lord of his life—has had this faith put inside him. You could not have been born again without it. *You have faith.* Now, for you to say or believe, "I don't have enough faith," or "I don't have any faith," is a slap in the face of the Word of God that says you do. Hebrews 12:2 says Jesus is the author and finisher of your faith. This faith is good enough to make all things possible to you, the believer. (See Mark 9:23.)

Let's make absolutely certain that what we have said is according to the Word. Remember, we have said that faith is born in the human heart at the time of conversion. So, every born-again believer has the faith of God in him *now*. We have said that the measure of faith in the heart of the believer is enough to do whatever it is called upon to do. Jesus is the author of our faith. Let's look at 1 John 5:1-5:

Whosoever believeth that Jesus is the Christ is born of God: and every one that loveth him that begat loveth him also that is begotten of him. By this we know that we love the children of God, when we love God, and keep his command-ments. For this is the love of God, that we keep his commandments: and his commandments are not grievous. For whatsoever is born of God over-cometh the world: and this is the victory that overcometh the world, even our faith. Who is he that overcometh the world, but he that believeth that Jesus is the Son of God?

Notice in verse 1 the word *whosoever.* This certainly means me and it certainly means you, if you believe that Jesus is the Christ. Now notice in verse 4 the word *what-soever.* These two words are referring to the same person. These verses tell us whosoever believes that Jesus is the Christ has enough victory faith in him to overcome the world. Just so there is no mistake about it, verse 5 asks the question, "Who is he that overcometh the world, but he that believeth that Jesus is the Son of God?" The Word has already said the power used to overcome the world is our faith. Think of it! There is enough of God's very own faith residing on the inside of you right now to overcome anything the world can throw at you!

God is a faith being. You are born of Him, so *you* are a faith being. God does not do anything outside of faith. With His faith living in you, you are to operate the same way.

Put on the whole armor of God and be strong in the Lord and in the power of *His* might (Ephesians 6:10-17). Put your faceplate down. That is God's suit you're wearing, and the devil can't tell you from Him when you are wearing His Name and His armor. He knows better than to tangle with God's armor because he has been so badly defeated by it. Resist him, and he *will* flee from you. He will run rapidly in the opposite direction. Always remember Satan does not have any weapon or device

greater than our faith. Ephesians 6:16 says the shield of
faith will quench *all* the fiery darts of the wicked. We
have God's Word for that. Now don't pull your faceplate
up and say, "I wonder if he went?" You just dropped
your shield of faith! Satan will know for sure that it isn't
God. He'll turn and jump right in the middle of you.
Wonderment will not take the place of faith.

Faith-Filled Words

And Jesus answering saith unto them, Have faith in
God. For verily I say unto you, That whosoever shall say
unto this mountain, Be thou removed, and be thou cast
into the sea; and shall not doubt in his heart, but shall
believe that those things which he saith shall come to
pass; he shall have whatsoever he saith (Mark 11:22-23).

In today's language this account would read some-
thing like this: "Jesus spoke to the fig tree, and it dried
up from the roots." In explaining it Jesus said, "This is the
way you operate the faith of God. You speak the desired
result and do not doubt in your heart. You believe that
your words have power, and the things you say will come
to pass. The result is that you can have whatever you say
when you believe."

Jesus said to believe that the *things* you say will come to pass. This doesn't mean you can continue to speak any way you want, and then in a time of need expect to exercise faith in God's Words. If you really believe faith words, you should speak them all the time.

You must change your vocabulary and discipline your speech so that your words are becoming to Jesus. *All* your words should be words of faith. You should only speak words you want to come to pass and believe they will produce results. By getting into the Word of God and continually feeding on it so faith controls our vocabulary, you can come to the place where all your words will come to pass. When your words are words of faith, God will be able to trust you with His power in the words of your mouth. What you speak, good or bad, is what you will receive.

Jesus said, "For out of the abundance of the heart the mouth speaks" (Matthew 12:34). The force of faith must be behind your words for them to cause things to come to pass. *You must believe in your heart.* Your mouth will speak what is put into your heart. If faith-filled words are put into your heart, faith-filled words will come out. If doubt and unbelief are put into your heart, words of doubt and unbelief will come out. Evil things out of an evil heart will come to pass. Words bring things to pass.

Your words work for you or against you. They enforce the law of sin and death, or they enforce the law of the Spirit of life (Romans 8:2).

The force of faith, then, is released in words. Faith-filled words put the law of the Spirit of life into operation. Faith-filled words dominate the laws of death and its forces ruled by Satan since the fall of Adam.

Jesus' faith-filled words raised a man from the dead. He said, *"Lazarus, come forth!"* (John 11:43). The man had been dead four days. He was bound hand and foot. The power in those words overcame death, picked Lazarus up and put life and healing into his decayed body (whatever killed him had to be healed). Faith-filled words brought Lazarus forth and set him outside the tomb, bound. *Then* men loosed him. Talk about faith-filled words!

How do you get words filled with this kind of power? Can you do it? The Word says, "Whosoever shall say unto this mountain...he shall have whatsoever he saith" (Mark 11:23). Yes, you can do it. Find out where faith comes from and go to work.

The Source of Faith

"So then faith cometh by hearing, and hearing by the word of God" (Romans 10:17). The Word of God produces faith in your heart. There is no other source of faith. Out of the abundance of the heart the mouth speaks. When you put faith-filled words—God's Word—into your heart, faith-filled words come out of your mouth. The Word has to be put in for faith to come out.

Faith is the product of your spirit. It comes into your spirit by hearing the Word and it is continually developed in your spirit by the Word.

Faith's results are determined by your confession, or what you say. Your confession corresponds to the level of the Word of God that is working in you. Romans 10:17 says, "Faith cometh by hearing, and hearing by the word of God." When you are filled with God's Word, faith comes up strong. When you neglect your study and meditation and become caught up in the affairs of life, you consume or use up the force of faith coming out of your spirit. Actually this process works in the spirit the same way it does in the physical body.

The physical body eats physical food and produces physical power called strength. The spirit of man feeds on spirit food and produces spirit power called faith. Jesus said, "The words that I speak unto you, they are spirit, and they are life" (John 6:63). They are *life!*

Proverbs 4:20-23 says: "My son, attend to my words; incline thine ear unto my sayings. Let them not depart

from thine eyes; keep them in the midst of thine heart.
For they are *life* unto those that find them, and health to
all their flesh. Keep thy heart with all diligence; for out
of it are the issues of life."

God's words are spirit and they are life. They are life
to your spirit. Faith comes by hearing the Word of God.
The force of faith issues out of your spirit and brings
life and health to your flesh. The Word not only brings
healing, but it keeps you healthy. Above all that you do,
keep your heart *full* of the Word because out of the heart
are the forces or issues necessary to live this life successfully. In other words, whatever you do, protect and
nourish your spirit. Feed it with the Word of God, and
the force of faith will issue out of it and work whenever
needed. You can understand why the Word says to keep
or to protect your heart with all diligence.

Faith, like any other force, must be applied in order to
gain any benefit from it. In the illustration we used about
the physical body, we can see that we eat physical food
and our body turns that food into strength. The strength
in the body then must be applied. It must be released. We
release our physical strength through action. In the same
way, the spirit man consumes spirit food (God's Word)
and that spirit food produces spirit power which is called
faith. Now, this faith force must be applied.

We have already discussed the releasing of faith and applying it with words. Faith is also released by acting on God's Word. James 1:22 says to be a doer of the Word. Jesus said in John 3:21, "He that doeth truth cometh to the light, that his deeds may be made manifest, that they are wrought in God." James 2:17 says, "Even so faith, if it hath not works, is dead." One translation says, "Faith without corresponding action will not work."

Begin by putting God's Word into your heart. As an act of your will, believe it. Then, say it with your mouth and act accordingly. You cannot continue to talk doubt and unbelief or act as though the Bible were not true. The Bible says, "God is our strength." (See Psalm 46:1.) So, begin to talk and act strong—even before you feel strong or look strong. The Bible says, "You are healed." Begin to talk healed and to act healed. The Bible says that God meets your need according to His riches in glory. Begin to talk as though it were true because *it is true!* This is faith receiving what God has already provided for us in Jesus.

Learn and develop this confession of faith: "I am not moved by what I see or by what I feel. I am moved only by what I believe. The victory is mine! I have it *now!* I can see it through the eye of my faith!"

2

Faith and Patience— The Power Twins

"My brethren, count it all joy when ye fall into divers temptations; knowing this, that the trying of your faith worketh patience. But let patience have her perfect work, that ye may be perfect and entire, wanting nothing" (James 1:2-4). "That ye be not slothful, but followers of them who through faith and patience inherit the promises" (Hebrews 6:12). The power of patience is a working power. When faith has a tendency to waver, it is patience that comes to faith's aid to make it stand. *The power of patience is necessary to undergird faith.* Almost everywhere you find faith mentioned in the Bible, you also find patience. Faith and patience are the power twins. Together they will produce every time. Patience without faith has no power to call into reality the things desired because faith is the substance of things we hope for. So, patience without faith has no substance.

Faith without patience, on the other hand, will often fail to stand firm on the evidence of the Word that gives deed to things not seen. Jesus told Peter that He had prayed for him that his faith would not fail. Without the power of patience at work, we will allow sense knowledge—the things we see—to overwhelm our faith that is based on what the Word says. *Patience undergirds faith and gives it endurance to persevere until the answer comes.* Faith is a powerful force. It always works. Not that our faith is weak and needs strength, but without the power of patience we ourselves stop the force of faith from working with negative confession and action. It is our faith, and we can put it into action or we can stop it from working.

Traditionally, we think of patience as knuckling under and being satisfied with whatever comes our way. That is not at all what patience is. Patience is a real force. It has to be developed. The Word says in Titus 2:2 that we are to be sound or developed in patience. Faith is a force that has to be developed. The same scripture says that we are to be sound in faith. Patience and faith are individual forces. They work together the way faith and love work together. All are distinct forces and play different roles in our Christian lives.

It is dangerous to confuse these forces and try to use one in the place of the other. For instance, the Bible says in Hebrews 11:1 that faith is the substance of things hoped for. Hope without faith has no substance.

People say, "We are hoping and praying." This sounds good but in this case, hope is being confused with faith. Without the substance of faith that kind of praying will not produce any results. You can see that in a critical situation this would be dangerous. We need to have our thinking straightened out according to the Bible so that we can properly use these forces to produce God's perfect will in our lives.

One of the most common traditions and mistakes in this area of believing is that trials and tribulations develop faith. Trials and tribulations do not develop faith... *faith cometh by hearing, and hearing by the Word of God.* Trials and tribulations develop patience. We have already learned from James 1 that this is true. The Apostle Paul says the same thing in Romans 5:3.

Faith is developed as we act on the Word of God. Hebrews 12:2 states that Jesus is the author and finisher, or developer, of our faith. It does not say that Satan is the developer of our faith. It is vitally important that we realize the difference between the developing of faith and the developing of patience.

Faith should be developed on the Word of God before the trial or testing comes. Jesus said in Luke 6:47-48 that if a man acted on His words, he would be like a man who built his house on a rock. When the flood beat upon the house, the house did not fall. Notice, in this scripture, the man had to dig deep. This is where his faith was developed. During the storm was when his patience was developed. He knew his house would stand because it was built on rock. Remember *how* Jesus said the man built on that rock? He acted on the Word. Faith is developed before the trial comes. The force of patience is developed in the trial or tribulation and undergirds or keeps the door open for faith to work and to overcome the situation.

The definition of *patience* is "being constant or being the same way at all times." James 1 says that we are to be single-minded. We must always respond or react in every circumstance of life the same way—on the Word of God. Regardless of what may be thrown at us, we must become so Word-of-God minded that we do not act in fear or doubt but always act on whatever the Word of our God says. The Word says that Jesus is the same yesterday, today and forever. Jesus has always and will always respond to the Word rather than to circumstances, reason or fear. This is the way that we should be. Being sound in patience is to answer every doubt and fear with the firm assurance and confession that God's Word is true, regardless of what we feel or see. Regardless of what storm may come our way, our Father's Word cannot fail. In that kind of atmosphere, faith is free to move and overcome whatever Satan has put in our way. James 1:12-21 says:

Blessed is the man that endureth temptation: for when he is tried, he shall receive the crown of life, which the Lord hath promised to them that love him. Let no man say when he is tempted, I am tempted of God: for God cannot be tempted with evil, neither tempteth he any man: but every man is tempted, when he is drawn away of his own lust, and enticed. Then when lust hath conceived, it bringeth forth sin: and sin, when it is finished, bringeth forth death. Do not err, my beloved brethren. Every good gift and every perfect gift is from above, and cometh down from the Father of lights, with whom is no variableness, neither shadow of turning. Of his own will begat he us with the word of truth, that we should be a kind of firstfruits of his creatures. Wherefore, my beloved brethren, let every man be swift to hear, slow to speak, slow to wrath: For the wrath of man worketh not the righteousness of God. Wherefore lay apart all filthiness and superfluity of naughtiness, and receive with meekness the engrafted word, which is able to save your souls.

To properly develop the power of patience, we must know what the Bible says about testings and trials. The Greek word translated *temptations* in these scriptures is the same word for *trials* and *testings*. It is vitally important that we know, from verse 13, that God is not tempted by evil, and He does not tempt or test men with evil. We are warned never to say that we are tested of God.

Verse 14 explains that a test or trial is anything that puts pressure on the lusts or desires of the flesh. *Any pressure that draws us away from God's Word is the beginning of a test.* If we then act on that lust, sin is the result. Still, we have a way of escape, for the Word says we have an advocate with the Father, Jesus Christ. He is faithful to forgive us our sins when we confess them.

We are still more than conquerors in Jesus. When Satan applies pressure to our bodies to make them sick, for example, we don't have to succumb to that pressure. When he presents us with financial ruin, we don't have to yield to the temptation to turn to the world and borrow. Most of the time, this only makes matters worse. Thank God, we can turn to God's Word in Philippians 4:19 and use our faith. Then, regardless of circumstances, we exercise the power of patience and continue to stand fast in the liberty to which we have been called.

Don't forget the ministry of the Holy Spirit in all of

this. He is continually working in you, teaching, interceding and backing your faith with His mighty power. This is where the power of patience is so very important. As long as your faith is active, the Spirit of God is active. It is impossible to please God without faith. Patience guards against admitting a doubt or confession of fear into your consciousness. Even when you stretch your faith as far as it will go, He who is within you is greater than he who is in the world.

First Corinthians 10:13 says, "There hath no temptation taken you but such as is common to man: but God is faithful, who will not suffer you to be tempted above that ye are able; but will with the temptation also make a way to escape, that ye may be able to bear it."

This scripture reveals three more important things about trials: (1) Testings and temptations are common to man. No man is ever tested or tried with things that are not common to mankind. Satan does not have the right to call upon his experience as a heavenly being to apply things as tests or trials that are outside the realm of humanity. (2) God is faithful. You will never face anything that you cannot overcome. (3) God always provides the way of escape.

Satan is limited to this earth realm and his weapons are no match for what God has provided for us. Thank

God, the weapons of our warfare are not carnal but powerful *through God* to the pulling down of strongholds (2 Corinthians 10:4). Satan is limited to the things that are common to mankind, but we are not. We have access to the full armor of God. Our patience rests solidly on the full assurance that, no matter what comes next, Jesus has provided more than enough victory to put us over.

Many Christians quote Romans 8:28 which says, "... all things work together for good to them that love God" as an excuse to fail. To them this scripture says, "All the devil does to me will turn out for my good. After all, you know the Bible says we are made stronger by the trials and tribulations of this life." The Bible does not say that at all! When the Apostle Paul wrote that all things work together for the good of those who love God and are called according to His purpose, he was teaching on intercessory prayer.

> Likewise the Spirit also helpeth our infirmities: for we know not what we should pray for as we ought: but the Spirit itself maketh intercession for us with groanings which cannot be uttered. And he that searcheth the hearts knoweth what is the mind of the Spirit, because he maketh intercession for the saints according to the will of God. And

we know that all things work together for good to them that love God, to them who are the called according to his purpose (Romans 8:26-28).

All things work together for the good of those who love God, when we are operating together in intercessory prayer!

While a friend and I were talking about prayer, the Lord said to me, *Those things do not mean all bad things work together for the good of those who love God. I am talking about the things of God: the Word of God, the gifts of the Spirit, the Name of Jesus and the power weapons of the Body of Christ. These are the things that work together for the good of those who love God.* Under this kind of operation, the things that the devil throws at you will be overcome by the power of the things of God, and victory will be the result.

Many trials that Satan causes make people weaker instead of stronger. If it were the trials and tribulations that made us strong, everyone on earth would be a spiritual giant. Certainly there have been enough trials and tribulations to perfect the saints. So, that must not be the avenue through which God perfects us.

"And he gave some, apostles; and some, prophets; and some, evangelists; and some, pastors and teachers; for the perfecting of the saints, for the work of the ministry, for the edifying of the body of Christ" (Ephesians 4:11-12).

This is the way the saints are perfected—*not* through tribulations. We are to be perfected by the Word through the ministry.

Well, I don't know about you, but I'm glad to know that God did not send cancer to edify me or poverty to perfect my faith. No, those curses are not from God. They are from Satan, and we are to triumph over them with the power twins—faith and patience.

The Word does not say that faith is developed by trials, but it does say that the trying of our faith worketh patience. It is what we do with trials and tribulations that makes the difference, not the fact that we are suffering. There are those in the Church who think we are to glory in tribulations. Tribulation is not the goal of Christianity. Many think that we cannot be worth anything until we suffer. That is not true. You will not be worth anything unless you *overcome* that suffering. Suffering is the result of the attack of Satan. There is no glory in knuckling down and enduring a trial. The glory is in overcoming that trial with the Word of God through the power of God. This is why we can count it all joy when we are tried. We know that Jesus has defeated Satan, and that we are victors over anything he sends our way.

Jesus said in John 16:33, "These things I have spoken unto you, that in me ye might have peace. In the world ye shall have tribulation: but be of good cheer; I have overcome the world." The glory lies in overcoming the world and its trials and tribulations. Trouble may come our way, but through the good things of God, He always causes us to triumph in Christ Jesus (2 Corinthians 2:14).

The Apostle Paul said, "Therefore being justified by faith, we have peace with God through our Lord Jesus Christ.... And not only so, but we glory in tribulations also: knowing that tribulation worketh patience; and patience, experience; and experience, hope" (Romans 5:1, 3-4). Paul was saying that he had peace with God whatever came his way. He had this peace, not only when things were working right for him, but also when trouble came down the road. He did not let go of his peace with God because of tribulation. It only worked patience in him, and *patience brought the experience of victory*. Then the experience of victory worked hope.

"Cast not away therefore your confidence (or faith), which hath great recompence of reward. For ye have need of patience, that, after ye have done the will of God, ye might receive the promise.... Now the just shall live by faith" (Hebrews 10:35-36, 38). Remember, he said in Romans 5 that tribulation works patience, and Hebrews 10 says that we have need of patience because patience works experience. Experience is the reward. Patience produces the reward of experiencing the answer.

"For ye have need of patience, that, after ye have done the will of God," or you could say it this way, that "after you have acted on the Word of God, employ the power of patience and you will receive the promise of that Word." Hebrews 6:12 tells us that through faith and patience we inherit the promises. Faith is acting on the Word. God's Word is His will. After you have exerted the force of faith by acting on the Word (the will of God), then patience comes into action to produce the experience of victory!

With the power of patience at work, the experience of faith's result is inevitable. If your body has symptoms of sickness, for example, it may be screaming with pain. You must get your faith into operation. The first thing you do is go to the will of God—the Word. Open your Bible to Matthew 8:17, "Himself took our infirmities, and bare our sicknesses." First Peter 2:24: "Who his own self bare our sins in his own body on the tree, that we, being dead to sins, should live unto righteousness: by whose stripes ye were healed." God's Word does not say that by His stripes you *may* be healed. First Peter 2:24 says "By whose stripes you were healed." It says, *You were healed.*

Now you are beginning to look at healing through the eye of faith. Your faith is looking beyond the symptoms in your body. Then you say, "Father, 1 Peter 2:24 says that by the stripes of Jesus, I was healed. I apply this Word to my body, and I command it to be healed in the Name of Jesus. The Word says that I am healed. I say that I am healed. Sickness, I speak to you in the Name of Jesus, and I command you to leave my body."

That did it. You believed you received when you prayed. Jesus said, "Therefore I say unto you, What things soever ye desire, when ye pray, believe that ye receive them, and ye shall have them" (Mark 11:24). You have His Word.

Many times all symptoms leave immediately, but not always. There are times when the power of patience must be put into operation to undergird your act of faith on God's Word. You did the will of God when you did what the Word says. Now you have need of patience so that you will be entire and wanting nothing. The experience of that healing is inevitable. It is not a "maybe it will and maybe it won't" situation. The Word says you were healed. Now through patience, you must hold fast to that Word concerning healing, regardless of symptoms or pain, knowing that patience *will* produce the experience of healing. Working the power of patience is the difference between success and failure in the faith walk.

"Now faith is the substance of things hoped for, the

evidence of things not seen" (Hebrews 11:1). You must believe that you are healed before you see the results in your body. You cannot wait until your body looks and feels healed before you believe it. If you do, you will never receive by faith. You cannot get faith's results without exerting the force of faith. Faith is believing that you receive whatever you ask *before* it can be seen or felt with the physical senses. You have the evidence. The Word of God is the evidence that you have it now, not the desired result.

You have exercised your faith in God's Word. Now let patience have her perfect work. The force of faith is at work, undergirded by the power of patience. Your faith connected with the Father the very moment you took His Word as the evidence of your healing. Now confess with your mouth that it is yours, and by your actions show that it is yours. You must talk healing, and act healing. Patience begins to work from the time you believed you received, and it must be allowed to work until the last symptom leaves your body. The voice of patience says, "I know God's Word is true. I will not be moved by what I see or feel. I will only be moved by the Word of God. I patiently rest on the truth of God's mighty Word!"

The experience of the answer is inevitable!

Prayer for Salvation and Baptism in the Holy Spirit

Heavenly Father, I come to You in the Name of Jesus. Your Word says, "Whosoever shall call on the name of the Lord shall be saved" (Acts 2:21). I am calling on You. I pray and ask Jesus to come into my heart and be Lord over my life according to Romans 10:9-10: "If thou shalt confess with thy mouth the Lord Jesus, and shalt believe in thine heart that God hath raised him from the dead, thou shalt be saved. For with the heart man believeth unto righteousness; and with the mouth confession is made unto salvation." I do that now. I confess that Jesus is Lord, and I believe in my heart that God raised Him from the dead. I repent of sin. I renounce it. I renounce the devil and everything he stands for. Jesus is my Lord.

I am now reborn! I am a Christian—a child of Almighty God! I am saved! You also said in Your Word, "If ye then, being evil, know how to give good gifts unto your children: HOW MUCH MORE shall your heavenly Father give the Holy Spirit to them that ask him?" (Luke 11:13). I'm also asking You to fill me with the Holy Spirit. Holy Spirit, rise up within me as I praise God. I fully expect to speak with other tongues as You give me the utterance (Acts 2:4). In Jesus' Name. Amen!

Begin to praise God for filling you with the Holy Spirit. Speak those words and syllables you receive—not in your own language, but the language given to you by the Holy Spirit. You have to use your own voice. God will not force you to speak. Don't be concerned with how it sounds. It is a heavenly language!

Continue with the blessing God has given you and pray in the spirit every day.

You are a born-again, Spirit-filled believer. You'll never be the same!

Find a good church that boldly preaches God's Word and obeys it. Become part of a church family who will love and care for you as you love and care for them.

We need to be connected to each other. It increases our strength in God. It's God's plan for us.

Make it a habit to watch the Believer's Voice of Victory Network and become a doer of the Word, who is blessed in his doing (James 1:22-25).

About the Author

Kenneth Copeland is co-founder and president of Kenneth Copeland Ministries in Fort Worth, Texas, and best-selling author of books that include *Honor—Walking in Honesty, Truth and Integrity*, and *THE BLESSING of The LORD Makes Rich and He Adds No Sorrow With It*.

Since 1967, Kenneth has been a minister of the gospel of Christ and teacher of God's Word. He is also the artist on award-winning albums such as his Grammy-nominated *Only the Redeemed, In His Presence, He Is Jehovah, Just a Closer Walk* and *Big Band Gospel*. He also co-stars as the character Wichita Slim in the children's adventure videos *The Gunslinger, Covenant Rider* and the movie *The Treasure of Eagle Mountain*, and as Daniel Lyon in the Commander Kellie and the Superkids™ videos *Armor of Light* and *Judgment: The Trial of Commander Kellie*. Kenneth also co-stars as a Hispanic godfather in the 2009 and 2016 movies *The Rally* and *The Rally 2: Breaking the Curse*.

With the help of offices and staff in the United States, Canada, England, Australia, South Africa and Ukraine, Kenneth is fulfilling his vision to boldly preach the uncompromised WORD of God from the top of this world, to the bottom, and all the way around. His ministry reaches millions of people worldwide through daily and Sunday TV broadcasts, magazines, teaching audios and videos, conventions and campaigns, and the World Wide Web.

Learn more about Kenneth Copeland Ministries
by visiting our website at **kcm.org**